Bryon

fr

Bryony Lavery's plays include *Bag*, *Origin of the Species*, *Witchcraze*, *Wicked*, *Kitchen Matters*, *Nothing Compares to You*, *Ophelia*, *A Wedding Story* and the award-winning *Her Aching Heart*. Her plays for young people include *More Light* and *Illyria*. Her extensive work for BBC Radio includes *No Joan of Arc*, *Velma and Therese*, *The Smell of Him*, *Requiem* and adaptations of *Wuthering Heights*, *High Wind in Jamaica* and *Lady Audley's Secret* for the Classic Serial. She has adapted *Behind the Scenes at the Museum* for York Theatre Royal and Angela Carter's *The Magic Toyshop* for Shared Experience. She is an honorary Doctor of Arts at De Montfort University. *Frozen* won the TMA Best Play Award in 1998 and the Eileen Anderson Central Television Award for Best Play in 1998.

Bryony Lavery

---

f r o z e n

ff

Faber and Faber

New York / London

Faber and Faber, Inc.
An affiliate of Farrar, Straus and Giroux
19 Union Square West, New York 10003

Faber and Faber Ltd
3 Queen Square
London WC1N 3AU

Library of Congress Control Number: 2003110340
ISBN: 0-571-21129-1

1   3   5   7   9   10   8   6   4   2

The author wishes to express her gratitude to Marian Partington, for her words and her courage.

Frozen was first performed at the Birmingham Repertory Theatre on 1 May 1998, with the following cast:

Nancy Anita Dobson
Ralph Tom Georgeson
Agnetha Josie Lawrence
Daughter Gloria Nicholls
Guard Matthew Seymour
Voice of David Nabkus Joel Kaplan

Directed by Bill Alexander
Designed by Ruari Murchison
Lighting by Tim Mitchell
Music by Jonathan Goldstein

Frozen was revised and revived in the Cottesloe Theatre at the National Theatre, London, on 25 June 2002, with the following cast:

Nancy Anita Dobson
Ralph Tom Georgeson
Agnetha Josie Lawrence

Directed by Bill Alexander
Designed by Ruari Murchison
Lighting by Paul Pyant
Music by Jonathan Goldstein

The revised version of the text is the one published here.

The American premiere of *Frozen* took place on March 18, 2004, at the East 13th Street Theater. It was produced by MCC Theater; Robert LuPone and Bernard Telsey, artistic directors. It was directed by Doug Hughes; sets were designed by Hugh Landwehr; costumes by Catherine Zuber; lights by Clifton Taylor; with original music by David Van Tieghem. The production stage manager was B. D. White. The cast was as follows:

Nancy	Swoosie Kurtz
Ralph	Brian F. O'Byrne
Agnetha	Laila Robins

Characters

Ralph

Nancy

Agnetha

Voice of David

Guard

frozen

Act One

ONE: FAREWELL TO NEW YORK

New York street sounds . . . busy, whirling traffic and voices. Stops abruptly as light reveals . . .
Agnetha, hallway of her apartment, New York. Checking her airline tickets, passport.

Agnetha
Yes
yes
yes
yup
yeah
yo.

All is ready. She looks around. Looks through a doorway.

Bye room.

Gives the room a little wave.

Bye bedroom.
Bathroom.
Office.

She salaams gravely.

Bye home.

They all get waves, thumbs up, high signs, as appropriate. Until . . . she's ready. She picks up airline tickets, carry-on bag. She's ready. Then, she unclenches her jaw . . . and her teeth start chattering.

Oh no.
I do not need this.

Not now.
Please.

*But it is now. She puts down her tickets. Her teeth
chatter uncontrollably. She succumbs loudly to the
chattering . . .*

Er g-g-g-g-g-g-g-g . . .
oo g-g-g-g-g-g-g . . .
okay
out
good.

*She waits again. Then tears fill her eyes and she starts
blubbing. She encourages herself to cry . . . then
bawl . . . there is something deliberate and good-
humoured about it . . . as if she is two people . . . one
expressing emotion, the other encouraging it out . . .*

Mmmmuuuuuuurrr . . .
mmmmmmaaaaaaaaaaa . . .
yes, come on . . .
wwwwwaaaaaaahhhhhhh . . .
mmmmmmaaaaaaaaaahhh . . .
Come on . . .
plane to catch . . .!
Oh boy . . .

*The bawling moves into keening and howling, so
Agnetha must pick up her carry-on bag, which she
screams into, muffling the sound somewhat. She
screams and screams. Finally . . .*

Okay.
Finished?
Finito?

She checks.

Yes.

4

Yep.
Okay.
Good.

Picks up her travel documents, bag etc., again.

Yes yes yes yup yeah yo . . .

She calls loudly through the walls.

Sorry, Mrs Lipke!
The Big Noise is leaving!
Sorry Mr Chen!
Crazy Horse is outta here!

She leaves for the airport.
The sound of a large plane flying over . . . heading
towards . . .

TWO: FAMILY LIFE

The gentle chirrup, hum, buzz of an English garden . . .
Nancy, home, her back garden, evening, idly nipping
buds off.

Nancy
I should have gone round myself with those secateurs.
We've never seen eye to eye on shrubbery.
I'm prune-to-a-dormant-bud
but she'll be instigating a slash-and-burn regime.
She's let her *Clematis montana alba* do its own thing.

I said 'They like their feet in the shade and their head in
the sun' but she's plonked it
in a south-facing bed
sandy soil
and it's gone on the rampage over into next door's
    speciality alpines.

I offered to go round myself tomorrow and cut it back
    for her
but she says 'It's Bridgnorth tomorrow.'
Always leaves it to the last minute and then it's got
    to be
done This Minute Now Immediately.
So I asked for volunteers but that was like getting
someone to sign up for active service . . .
Bob's got Nautilus training . . .
and what's *that* all about . . .?

A plane flies overhead. Nancy 'tuts' gently.

Been very happy with his flab till now
and I always say 'I'm very partial to your love handles'
when we have a cuddle
but
well
so I need one of the girls to look lively.
But Ingrid's 'off' Grandma at the moment because of
The Make-Up Question
so I think easier all round if I send Rhona . . .
but Rhona's so good I always put on her
and I try to be fair
so I gird my loins to tackle Ingrid
in spite of it being like negotiating with Attila the Hun
    these days . . .
I've taken a Deep Breath . . .
when suddenly Crash Bang Wallop
Holy War breaks out upstairs! . . .
'What Is It Now?' . . . I go – and that's when Bob
    slithers out . . .
I hear the door click shut as I get up the stairs . . .
he's so . . . *sneaky* these days . . .
no 'Goodbye then Nancy love . . .'
well.
In The War Zone . . .

There's a Max Factor Thick-Lash mascara wand
gone missing from Attila's *private* drawer
and who's Suspect Number One . . . ?
Ingrid goes into Rhona's room
to obligingly fetch her for me,
drags her back by her *hair*, so I *separate* them
and look at the Young One.

She smiles.

She looks like a panda!
Great black-rimmed eyes.
I say to Ingrid 'Go on, give her a bamboo shoot.'
wrong thing to say . . .
'Mum! Rhona's not *funny*!
You should take this *seriously*.'
I say 'Who takes *me* seriously about a ceasefire on
this Fighting?'
and I pop in 'So . . . Ingrid, why don't you go round to
Grandma's for a bit of peace?'
and she's almost hooked when I add . . . 'And you
    could take
the secateurs while you're at it . . .'
and she's off again. 'I'm just an unpaid skivvy in this
establishment . . . I wish I was an orphan . . . I wish
    somebody
would adopt me . . . nobody loves me . . .
everybody loves Rhona best . . .'
I say hopefully 'Now stop that nonsense . . .
I love you both equally in different ways.'
I don't.
I don't love either of them *at all* at the moment!
Or Bob!
Or Mother!
Any of them!
They can all go to hell for all I care.

Quite close by, a van accelerates . . .

But anyway
somehow it happenes
Ingrid has me agreeing to let her go out
to 'Co-work on a joint domestic sciences project'
that involves wearing *full* Warpaint
with Jez or Maz or Spaz or somebody . . .
and chain of command's put the youngest soldier on
secateur duty!
Little Panda.
My mother's going to think I'm letting *her* wear
makeup too young and be Reading The Riot Act!!! . . .
That's probably why Rhona's not back yet.
Time!
Yes!!!

THREE: A BAD PATCH

Ralph, in his room, washing his hands at a sink.

Ralph
You know

it's one of those days
you're just going to do it
you might do it.
I suppose mostly I'm a bit of a cold fish.

He dries his hands carefully on a small, clean towel.

But then, these times
things hot up.
It's been a bit of a bad patch for me . . .
fucking landlady . . .
pardon my French . . .
despite I told her I don't eat lamb . . .
despite I told her I'm not a big eater . . .
despite I made that clear . . .

turns up on the plate
and I've eaten it before I've said
'This isn't lamb is it . . .?'
and it *was* . . .

*Takes a small bottle of hand lotion, pours a dollop on
one palm, starts to rub it into both hands.*

And I've gone out with
hoojit . . . Raymond Quantock . . .
and that wassname from work . . . Dick Bottle . . .
and I've kept up with them putting it away . . .
otherwise . . .
and drunk five lager tops
and two . . . (*Counts in his head.*) . . . four . . .
Jack Daniels
and I've gone over on that damn foot again . . .
lightning strike of pain . . .
and it's put me in a strop
nobody better mess me with
nobody better
been like . . . offish
and . . .

He's on a street somewhere.

I just see her
and decide
I'm going to get her in the van.
I just want to keep her for a bit
spend some time with her.
I just do it.
It's a rush of blood.
Hello.

I said 'Hello'
are you deaf?
It's rude to ignore people.
Are you loony?

You're loony.
I'm only being polite.
No need to get the hump.
Not with me.
I just said 'Hello.'
Hello.
Hello.
Hello.
I'm saying 'hello' to you.
Least you can do is make conversation.
Kind of world is this
folk can't be sociable?
Polite.
Least you can do is make a response.
It's Bad Manners if you don't.
Bad manners.
Rude.
I said 'Hello.'
Hello.
Hello.
Hello.
Hello.
Hello then . . .
finally . . .
finally . . .
she goes
'Hello.'

I think she quite liked me.

Oh yes
she was interested.

The van's down here
obviously
the back door's not locked
because I've thought ahead
obviously

she wants to come
it's only fifty yards
it's convenient.

I've got cushions in the back
And a sleeping bag.
Obviously.

Sometimes you're fucked by
circumstances
things don't go your way.

Picks something up. Regards it.

The secateurs
I don't bargain for
but
in the event
they turn out
useful
and add to it all
passing off
efficiently
but
logistically
she's persuaded it's time
to get in the van
you make it work
she's in the van.

A sound of deliberate snipping of plants . . .
    He puts the top on the bottle of hand lotion.
Secures it.

Lovely evening.
Sunny . . . but with a light southerly breeze . . .

Nancy, Rhona's bedroom, seven months later . . .
a window overlooking the garden.

Nancy
 This is Leo. (*a small, threadbare soft-toy lion*)

 She smiles slightly.

 He's bald where she played Hairdressers on him.
 'Rhona's Rough Cuts.'

 Ingrid's making me a cup of coffee.
 She's like the Catering Corps these past few days.
 Mum, do you want a cup of hot chocolate?
 Mum, shall we have a milky drink?
 Mum, Cherry Bakewell?

 I've lost nearly two stone.

 I've gone back to smoking.
 Cast-Iron Excuse.
 Even my mother has to let me.

 It's bad today because it's Rhona's
 birthday tomorrow and they say
 Missing Children often phone on their
 birthdays.
 Get in touch . . .

 She holds her stomach. Swallows.

 So I thought
 clean her room
 her Nature Table's a bit dusty.

 Give me something to do.

 When she comes back
 everything will be nice

everything be the same
everything familiar.

That's gorse
with some sheep's wool tangled in it
from Brecon Beacons.
I got stuck between a lamb and its mother
the mother *ran* at me . . .
I ran like billy-o
the girls fell over laughing!
Rhona found this in the gap . . .
we had cheese-and-chutney sandwiches.

A cold wind blows . . .

Brecon Beacons.
She loved that day!
Wales! She's maybe . . . (*Thinks.*)
No. We leafleted Wales.

This is her witch stone
it's a witch stone if it has a
natural hole in it.
See.

Looks through it.

You can see things in a witchy way . . .
it's magic.

Holds it tightly in her hand, eyes tight closed. Making a wish.

Kept it there.

Mmm.

Puts it back exactly.

What are you doing on here, Leo?

You live on the bed!

Somebody's been in here . . .
maybe Bob . . .
to primp and preen in private!
I know what's going on and
I know who with.
It's all gone a bit softly-softly and undercover
what with The Disappearance . . .
but if it's over I'm Raquel Welch!

I don't care!

These books are different.

Ingrid!

It is stifling her . . .

Washing up
cleaning
doing
helping!
Well it's not!
I don't want anyone in here moving her things
round, I want to keep it exactly as it was!
If I have to get Bob to put a lock on that door
I will!

Rhona

where are you?

I know you're somewhere!

FIVE: MOVING ON

Ralph brings a suitcase into his room.

Ralph
That incident up Scotland
not down to me.

I operate in a southwards direction
Midlands Leicester Home Counties

Not fucking Scotland
Not cold icy windy Scotland!
Anybody with a *brain* would know that's Too Far!
Too far from my centre of operations.
I mean you're looking at transportation
something what over two hundred miles . . .
where's the sense in that?
Where's the efficiency?
You've got to keep things *clean* in every sense.
I don't touch *anything* outside an eighty mile radius
of my centre of operations.
Oh no
oh no
once you've got a site sorted
well, you don't mess with *that*, do you?
Obviously
but
mud sticks.

You've got to be fly in this game!
£750 for the van.
Him who bought it
didn't notice the chassis's all rust.
I've run it a coupla times through
that field near Uttoxeter. A518.
Stuck together with mud
fuck him if he can't make a thorough check!

I'll get something a later reg.
That's been a bit of an unlucky vehicle for me.
So's this place.
Landlady . . .
despite when the Old Bill come here
they found nothing
despite it's clean

despite I'm clear
despite that . . .
has gone 'Sling your hook
don't want you here
go
clear off . . .'
and I've no comeback on it in law!
Cunt
Fucking Cheek! . . . scuse me!
Kept it like a New Pin!

Who do they think they are?

Should be a law.
You should have a guarantee of security
for your money.

Good job I done planning here.
Good job I thought logistically . . .
had these in lock-up.

Taps head.

You've got to wake up very early to get ahead of me!
Oh yes!
Oh yes!

Videos are packed, titles mostly upright. He turns one round. Takes out a notebook. Refers to it.

Lollitots
Lesbian Lolita
Little Red Riding Hood

Beautiful, romantic, yearning music . . . sounds of summer countryside.

Little Ones in Love
Child Love
Lesbian Lolita at School

He turns a video the right way round . . . mock
exasperation . . . he loves these videos.

Lolita's Examination
Lolita's Auntie
Pre-Teen Trio

Sweet Patti
Sweet Susan
Little Linda
Baby Bonnie . . .

These cost!
What!!!
So I put them in safe storage
obviously.
Protect my investment.
I've had to get these from abroad!
Amsterdam, some of these!
France.
Denmark.

Nobody's having these

they're precious
oh yes
oh yes

I'm going to have to safekeep these in
my centre of operations
until I get a new residence.
I'm going to have to get some sort of
protective filing system.
I'm not sure that shed's efficient
dampwise . . .

He makes a short list.

Now I'm moving on

new start

oh yes
oh yes

A car drives off. Overhead, steady thrum of plane as . . .

SIX: THIS FLIGHT TONIGHT

Agnetha, on an aeroplane, laptop on her lap, keying sporadically . . . also drinking from a plastic cup . . .

Agnetha (*keys*)
  'Serial Killing . . . a forgiveable act?'

She drains her drink. Presses the 'Flight Attendant' summoning light . . . no response . . .

(*keys*)
  'Judicial Revenge . . . a political choice?'

Pours non-existent drops of liquid from two or three small inflight bottles of brandy into the glass. Presses 'Flight Attendant' call again . . . no response.

(*keys*)
  'Brandy Refill . . . a Forlorn Hope?'
  Yes . . . I think so . . . Close File . . . Save? . . . Oh yes
    please . . .
  Shit . . . e-mail . . . oh yes please . . .

She starts writing furiously . . .

Dear David,
Dearest Damn Fuck You Then David
Dear Doctor David Nabkus
I hate hate hate hate hate you.
All the people on this flight are in mortal danger and
it is your fault.
You will be responsible for these multiple deaths
as we plummet out of the sky

into the sea a very very very long way down there
right under where I am sitting.
On *big* air
over *big* sea
it is your fault
you and your Big News
you and your Hilarious Damn Bad Behaviour have
cast doubt upon probability
and alchemised me into
Miss Fudge Feeling of Washington Square
who is shit-scared of flying!
Give me back my real brain!
Hand over my native intelligence!
When we crash
because of you
because of you taking away my faith in anything
    at all . . .
I take innocent people with me . . .
Lily-White Souls perish here . . .

She pours a non-existent drop of brandy into her
glass.

Although the stewardess serving me deserves to die . . .
a lonely, painful, lingering, agonising death
for the impressive number of
times she has wilfully ignored my request for brandy
and for a certain radiant spitefulness over her
inability to provide me with a vegetarian meal . . .
I imagine pouncing,
sinking my teeth into her neck just above her
white pretty blouse and biting out her throat
murmuring all the time
'How's *this* for going with
The Meat Option?'

She covers her laptop screen with a 'don't copy my
homework' arm, against her next-door neighbour.

I believe their uniforms are stain resistant.

Looks out of the window.

Still over sea.
Watery death for us all then . . .
unless I cannabalise that fucking air-hostess bitch! . . .

Lovely, violent inflight movie.
Many good and worthless men perished
in explosions of bright red blood.

I thought of you.

Her eyes fill. She wipes them surreptitiously, then . . .

You bastard
you make me frightened of everything!

*The plane flies on. Ping of 'Fasten seat belts' sign
flashing on . . .*

Oh my God!

Reads computer.

SEND?
Why not?

The plane flies on.

SEVEN: FLAME

Nancy, smart suit, drink, her house, four years later.

Nancy
It always works . . .
but it was magnificent tonight!

I get whoever's in charge of introducing
to say quite simply . . .
'From the organisation *FLAME* . . .

Mrs Nancy Shirley . . .'
and I find if you just give it a minute
. . . they settle . . .
and then I go . . .

She is in a school hall, many silent people.

Ladies and gentlemen of the . . .
and I fill in where we are . . .
tonight it was a Parent/Teachers thing
in Spalding . . .
Ladies and gentlemen of the *whatever* . . .
on April 17th, 1980,
my daughter,
Rhona . . .

and I pick up her photograph . . .

walked out of my house
to go to her grandma's house.
She never got there
she never came back
she was ten.
She's been missing for
five years.
She will be fifteen years old tonight.
I know she's alive.
I have Faith.
Every night I pray
that whatever reason is stopping her coming home
will be removed
and that she'll phone
or write
or just knock on the door
and say 'Mum, it's me.'

Bob says he always watches that bit
it gives him a chill down his back he says.
I've got him giving me lifts to these dos

it's brought us closer together,
cemented us
along with us both getting Belief . . .
Stopped that nonsense
with that Nautilus trainer woman
I've got him on jogging . . .
he said 'When you showed our Rhona's
photograph tonight, I thought, we're going
to get lucky this time . . .'

and then I pick up the *other* photograph
and go . . .

This . . .
is Robert Greaves.
He disappeared on his way to
Boy Scouts on September 14th, 1976.
He was fourteen.
Today's his birthday . . .

You could have heard a *pin* drop . . .

He's twenty-three . . .
And four weeks ago he walked through
his parents' front door in Braintree, Essex
and said 'Mum, I'm back.'
because we at *FLAME* found him!
Even though my little girl
my Rhona is still out there
I *rejoice* for Mr and Mrs Greaves
that our organisation
was able to reunite them
with their Robert . . .

and Bob has the leaflets ready . . .
because *FLAME* is about
just that . . .
keeping that flame of hope alive
keeping it burning

so that our missing children
can see its light
and feel its warmth
and come towards it!

It's funny
I feel I was born to do this
I found nothing so easy to do as this
it's funny
but this is when I feel most alive . . .

Returns to her room.

So . . .
I'm not best pleased to get back to a
legless Ingrid
ashtray piled
another fag burn on the settee arm . . .
She says
'I had a bad dream
I'm in the frozen frozen Arctic
and I'm exploring
but I'm no good at it
I've lost somebody
the body's under the ice
but where
I walk
looking for . . .
but it's getting harder and colder
the ice is building up . . .'
I say 'No wonder, you've let the thermostat
go off . . .'
but she *wails* like a great soft thing . . .
says . . .
'I look for a hole
I look for a seal hole
but there's no hole
the body's down there

but it's all getting whiter.'

Pause.

I say 'Well never mind, do you want some
drinking chocolate?'
but she's off again
'But do you know what I do then?'

and I say 'No, what'
and she laughs

daft mad laugh
and says
'Oh
I go inside of course
to get warm.'

Pause.

Bloody girl!

Bloody girl!

*A confused explosion of time markers . . . New Year
bells . . . bonfire fireworks . . . Christmas.
   Time passing . . . clocks.*

EIGHT: TATTOO YOU

*Ralph, summer shirt, bench. He has tears in his eyes.
Twenty years later.*

Ralph
   Oya
   Oya
   Oya.

Limping . . . sits down, rubbing his ankle.

Fuck . . . this fucking hurts!

Stinging!
Oya!
But you got to suffer for something worthwhile!

Oh yes
oh yes.

*Pulls up his trouser leg, down his sock . . . reveals a
fresh tattoo.*

This is The Grim Reaper
seventy-five quid
three hours twenty-three minutes
two needles
five colours!
It's not rubbish this!
it's a traditional design
big with bikers
you get sickle *and* scythe.
Brilliant.

'The Needlemaster' in Burley.
Good service.
Cup of tea if you want
and clean
spanking clean.

Not like
(*contempt*) 'Body Art Tattooing, Dersingham'!

Shows a tattoo on his right arm.

Sunburst Dagger of Death.
Got done December for Christmas . . .
needler's a fucking woman . . .
'Gazza's booked. I'm registered.
Take it or leave it . . .'

Suppressed rage.

Well, I couldn't come back

obviously . . .
so . . .
she's jabbing and poking . . .
one hour forty-three minutes . . .
came up like a balloon!
Cunt!

Tattoo on forearm.

Compared to
this.

Can't remember.

This.

Aw. Shit . . .

Strokes tattoo.

Madonna and Child
four colours . . .

Herculean struggle to remember . . .

Tattoo Shack!

The Tattoo Shack!
Bridgnorth. A456.

Ex-biker
three hours forty . . .
fucking craftsman!

Other arm, forearm . . .

Chuck's Custom Tattoos.
I'm not happy with that.
Too plain.
I'm going to get it adorned

Upper arm . . .

as this.
I designed that.

That's an original.
Angels fighting Devils.
With Leafy-Tree background.
(*quoting*) 'Your design or mine.
Call now or just pop in.
Thousands of designs to choose from
professional and friendly.' A4112.
Sacred Art . . . Beominster, this one.

Good.

Rubs his newly tattooed ankle again.

Oya.
Oya.
Oya.

I'm going to have to take my mind
off this.

He stands up, flexing his foot.

Oh yes
oh yes
don't wanna be feeling this all the way back.

Somebody to talk to
spend a bit of time with
would be ideal
obviously.

Sun's hot.

Sees something . . . becomes very still, focused.

Hello.
I said 'Hello'.
Hello.
Hello.
Hello.

A young girl laughs somewhere . . .

NINE: CHICKENS COMING HOME

Nancy walking, three or four days later.

Nancy
Sun's so hot.

Four days ago
phone call from the police
they think they have some news for us
can they come over?

Terrible terrible restlessness anxiety
then two young policemen . . . *lads* . . .
one with fine soft hair like a kiddie's . . .
other lovely polished shoes
pitch up
say . . .
'We have apprehended a man in the
unsuccessful attempted abduction of a young girl . . .
subsequent inquiries have uncovered a lock-up shed
the earth floor contains the remains of other children
the man is now giving us names
one of them'

he says

'is Rhona.'

*Sound of great ice floes breaking up, cracking,
churning . . .*

I wanted to go out for a walk
up a hill somewhere

find some fresh air
there's no air.

Message
after message

after message
on the answerphone.
Newspapers
we must we must we must
want to talk to them.

Ingrid rings
comes over
makes something with noodles
can't touch it
but I show willing
twirl it around on the plate a bit with a fork.
Ingrid says
'Try with chopsticks . . . I'll show you how to . . .'
but I leave it all sitting there
dumped on the plate

puts me in mind of worms

I've given Bob some more paracetamol
his headache's approaching Gale Force . . .

All this time
I've been growing her up
she's been
he's had her buried away . . .

I wish this weather would break.

I wish it would pour it down.
It's unbearable.

Great Big Storm.

A huge storm breaks . . .

Ralph, a cell.

Ralph (*hand between his legs*)
  Piss!
  Shit!

They've just come the questions
all the time
all the . . . relentless
without thinking you might need a break
bit of time to think, collect your thoughts . . .
so
obviously
when this fucking woman policeman cunt
comes the nice the interested the . . .
'Those are interesting tattoos,
did you get them all done in the same place?'
I'm not thinking I'm not sharp enough
logistically to understand
that they're putting me in the frame in
the picture in the *area* for
the incidents!

Sunburst Dagger of Death
logged
date
area
fucking woman needler
places me in the area where the
dark-haired little . . .

Same
Tattoo Shack, Bridgnorth
kid in the shorts . . .
I was there
Madonna and Child.

Really, statistically,
once they put that information
with my petrol book and receipts
and the real slip-up in terms of
efficiency over this latest incident . . .
I've got to let them take me on it!

They get the shed
centre of my operations
they get my special videos
so
I admit
helpful
polite
so
how come then
they're taking turns with the whispering and threats . . .
You're not a man
that's not a man
you're going to have to have ears in your neck, boy
in your shoulders in your arse
every second in here
when you eat
think what we've put in there
think about it
and think about bum and knob and what
comes out of there boy . . . smegma come wank-juice
. . . I mean, the language . . .
and even when you're locked up alone don't sleep,
boy, because all around you we're lying eyes
wide open thinking what next what idea next
for you losing your eye say getting your knob
sliced like a breakfast sausage
somebody shoving somming like this . . .
up your smelly arse till you shit blood
snot in your food
don't ever rest don't ever sleep

yes, you keep your head down, boy
you keep flicking those eyes about
till we get you!

not on!
Oh no
oh no.

ELEVEN: NEAR

Nancy, by a window, looking out.

Nancy
    Kept my hair appointment
    I wanted it shaved
    I wanted it shaved
    some sign
    some sign
    tear my clothes
    I have it cut quite short.
    News interrupts the radio music
    in the salon.
    As she's cutting my hairdresser says
    'What d'you think of these awful goings on then?'
    Does she really want to know?

    Police
    the fair tufty-haired one said . . .
    there's something you should know . . .
    something he's said . . .
    where he took her . . .

    That shed on Far Forest Lane
    he took her there
    all the time we were first looking
    she was just over there.

    I went past it!

How many times?

Not on her way to my mother's at all
there
if I'd thought earlier
got up from *gardening* earlier
gone down there
spotted a light
heard a – oh sound
seen across there
something that made me go across
investigate

she must have known how near I was
if she'd made a noise
I could have heard her I think
oh
all night
something heavy
block of ice
burning ice
pressing on my lungs

oh
oh . . .

A sound of clapping . . .

TWELVE: LOVELY TO BE HERE

Agnetha, a large, academic hall somewhere.

Agnetha
Oh
oh
oh
well thank you!
What a warm reception!

Thank you!
I'm very touched. Sincerely.
It's terrific to be here!
England. I'm honoured.
London. I'm touched.
Ladies and gentlemen . . .
Please. Now . . .
Let me repay you for your very generous Visiting
Fellowship by . . .
So . . .
Let's see me earn my bucks!

*She gets business-like. Takes up a place behind a
lectern. Notes. A screen backs up what she is saying.*

The title of my thesis is
'Serial Killing . . . a forgiveable act?'
and it is a critical examination of the differences
between crimes of evil
and crimes of illness.
I will base my critique upon
A psychiatric and neorological study of
the criminal brain conducted by myself and colleagues
during my tenure as
Amex-Suntori Chair of Psychiatry
New York School of Medicine . . .

Okay
the personal stuff . . .
My name is Dr Agnetha Gottmundsdottir . . .
My ancestors came to America
from a small frozen very cold ice-bound
place which experiences for a lot of the time
perpetual night . . .
so I guess it is in my Icelandic genes to want to take
myself and you, in my thesis . . .
to explore just such a frozen place . . .
But I am a *psychiatric* explorer.

34

So my chosen expedition will be . . .
the Arctic frozen sea that is . . .
the criminal brain.

Ralph's head lit as if it is an exhibit.

Let us take a look.

She walks over to stand behind Ralph, demonstrating
around his head, but not touching.
    A prison guard stands some way off, watching.

The cortex is the thick covering of grey
matter on the upper part of every
human brain
and the function of the cortex
and in particular
those parts of the cortex
beneath the forehead known as
the frontal lobes
is to modulate the impulses that surge up
from within the brain.
The cortex and the frontal lobes
are there to provide judgement,
to organise behaviour
and decision-making
to learn and stick to
rules of everyday life.
Ladies and gentlemen . . .
they are responsible for making us human.

I intend here to examine
what goes wrong with that humanity . . .
which can make certain individuals appear inhuman
using data collected from case studies
conducted by myself and colleagues
in New York and California
over the last ten years
plus my present case work here in England.

Ralph Ian Wantage
is currently in Long Lartin Maximum Security Prison
serving a life sentence without remission
for the abduction, sexual assault
and murder of seven young girls
over a period of twenty-one years . . .

*The light on Ralph extends. Agnetha and Ralph are
in the same space.*

Ralph
Cunt.

Agnetha
Doctor.
Let us be polite with one another, mm?

Ralph
I can be polite.
I've got manners.
I'm a gentleman.
Oh yes.
Oh yes.

Agnetha
Yes.
Good.
May I measure the circumference of your head?

*Ralph assents . . . big accommodating gesture. As she
measures his head, he sniffs her.*
    She writes.

Ralph
Cunt.

Agnetha
No.
I think probably Chanel Number 19

and a mild and gentle soap.
Stop being dangerous, Ralph.

Ralph
If you know my name,
you know my reputation.

Agnetha
Sure I do.
Can you hold your hands apart
like . . .
and spread your fingers . . .
good . . .

He copies her.

Agnetha
Interesting tattoo.

Ralph
Oh no, clever cunt.
What you after?

Agnetha
I'm looking for discontinuous,
jerky little movements . . .

As his fingers, arms jerk . . .

Ah-ah.

She holds up a finger, 45 degrees to his left.

Would you let your eyes
follow my finger, please . . .?

His eyes follow jerkily.

Ralph
Oh . . .! Shite.

She stops.

Agnetha
Can we try that again . . .
can you try to watch it go smoothly across . . . ?

Tries it again. Jerky again.

Ralph
Shite.

Agnetha
Okay. Good.
Now look at the ceiling.
Just with your eyes . . .

He cannot.

Ralph
Shite.
This has got to stop!

Agnetha
I'm sorry.
Just . . .
please stay still . . .
(*to Guard*) It's okay . . .
I'm just going to . . .

She goes behind him, reaches over the top of his head, he starts . . .

Ralph
Hey, no way!

Agnetha
. . . touch him . . .
I'm sorry, I did not mean to startle you!
I'm not gonna harm you.
I'm gonna tap you on the nose . . .
Just let me . . .

She taps a rhythm on the bridge of his nose. He blinks rapidly, gets distressed as . . .

Ralph
Hey
hey
hey
hey . . .

Sound of girl laughing . . .
  Lights down on Ralph as Agnetha moves away . . .
showing us on her own nose.

Agnetha
When you tap someone on the
bridge of the nose, it's reasonable
for the person to blink a coupla times
because there is a threat from outside.
When it's clear there is no threat . . .
a person should be able to accommodate that.
But if the subject blinks more than three times,
that's what we call 'insufficiency of suppression'
which may show frontal lobe disfunction.
The inability to accommodate
means you can't adapt to a new situation.

There's a certain rigidity there

like the person is ice-bound

in a kinda Arctic midwinter.

THIRTEEN: SUFFER

Nancy, smoking, her house.

Nancy
I'd like to see him die
watch him
suffer.
he wouldn't suffer like she suffered

39

but it would be something.
An eye for an eye
tooth for a tooth
I want to see that.

Everybody at *FLAME*'s
been very understanding.
The committee were in absolute agreement
when I suggested we shifted focus
from missing persons . . .
to spotlight an even more crucial area of
community responsibility . . .
Paedophile Identification . . .
Marjorie Alexander pressed my arm
and said 'We're with you two hundred per cent.'
When I get up now
and say

'If we had known
ladies and gentlemen
that within a few hundred yards of us
in a rented lock-up shed
there was a known convicted paedophile . . .
we would have been vigilant
we would have been forewarned
we would have been able to protect our little girl . . .'

the clapping is always tumultuous
people always stand up
a few at first
then it's a full-blown ovation . . .
we're tapping into something very, very deep here.

I got back tonight
somebody from an affiliated organisation's
sent me a video.
America
they've got a scheme

you can go and be there when they die
murderers.
You get a run-up visit
they show you the electric chair
how it all works
they take you through the procedure
the warders were *very* sympathetic . . .
the enforcement workers always are . . .
and then, you can be present,
members of victims' families
at that final moment.

He doesn't suffer like she suffered
but it would be something.

A sound of lightning connecting with earth source . . .

There was a *grandmother* on the video . . .
eighty-something, she went . . .
little grandkiddy shot stone-dead by a killer . . .
she goes
(*bad American accent*) 'I kin fergive,
but I kain't fergit.'
Talk about guts!
(*English*) I can forgive,
but I can't forget.
Mother says . . .
'I'm a forgiving woman
but I can't forgive what he's done.
I'd be there, Nancy, I'd be there . . .'

Bob says 'I'd be there'
I said 'If you were there, you'd go for him.'
He says 'I would . . . if there were a window of
opportunity, I'd be through it . . .'
He would.

Pause.

All through this, not a peep out of Ingrid.
Eating from a big economy bag of crisps.
Size of her since she gave up her smoking
and drinking!
Hasn't thought to hand them round.
Just . . . hugs the bloody bag to herself . . .
chomping . . .
suddenly . . . she says
'I'm going off.
Travelling.
I thought India, Nepal.
The East.'

Why?

Why?

Mosquitoes.
Noise.
People.
Coloured.
Foreign.

*Sound of a busy street market/bazaar . . . foreign
voices . . . business . . .*

Disease.
Lice.
Malaria.
Danger.
Hot.
Filth.
Dirt.
I don't care.

FOURTEEN: FOUR FARM FUCK

Agnetha, with Ralph, prison. Guard on duty.

Agnetha
Okay. Good.
Give me as many words as you can
that begin with . . .
F.

Ralph
Four.
Fourteen.
Forty-four.

Pause.

Farm.
Farm.
Farming.
Farming.
Farm.
Farm.

Pause.

Fuck.
Fucker.
Fucking.

He is pleased with these.

Fuck.

Agnetha
Any more, Ralph?

Ralph
Four.
Fourteen.
Forty-four.

Pause.

Four.

Agnetha
You've said that, Ralph . . .

Ralph
I'm not fucking stupid!
I'm not fucking stupid you know . . .

Agnetha (*pats his arm*)
Shhh.
It's alright.
It's not an intelligence test.
You do very well in intelligence tests.
You're not stupid.

As she walks away from him . . .

. . . you're manipulative and intense and
kinda mesmerising like a *rattlesnake* and you're a
  multiple
killer and I'd just really like a cigarette suddenly
but you're not . . .

Into lecture hall . . .

This is not an intelligence test.
If I asked Ralph to list . . . say . . . sixteen products
he might buy in a supermarket . . .
he would do just as well as anyone else . . .

Ralph
Beans, lamb chops, pizza, potatoes, Smash,
biscuits, lager, whisky, apples, carrots,
crab sticks, steak . . . hamburgers . . . pop tarts
(*Etc. and on . . . as . . .*)

Agnetha
That is a structured test,

44

with familiar objects.
The word-fluency test I have done asks
the testee to cope with situations
where there are no rules,
where they have to improvise,
where they make unfamiliar associations.
My colleague David Nabkus and I have
been conducting these tests for over twenty years . . .

Pause.

Sorry.
Something in my eye.
Sorry.

Ralph
Economy sausages
fish fingers
frozen peas.

Agnetha
And

Normal is fourteen, give or take . . .
Anyone who does less than nine . . .
is abnormal.
And falls within mine and David Nabkus's study.

We believe Ralph is abnormal
and we believe we can show you
the reason why . . .

for what that's worth

hey David?

FIFTEEN: ABSOLUTELY NOTHING

Sound of machinery . . .

Nancy
  Somebody from the newspaper rang up
  told Bob
  said
  'That shed
  where they found Rhona and the others
  where he . . .
  they're going to have it down
  they're going to flatten it . . .'
  I started to . . .
  I got . . .
  stomach ache all across . . . (*bowel area*)

  Workman tartan check shirt
  came and knocked
  said
  'Mrs Shirley . . . we're going to have it down for you
  that shed
  do you want to come and watch?'
  I said
  'I do.'

  We walked
  it's no distance
  and . . .

  Nearer machinery . . . engines . . .

  big mechanical digger . . .
  demolition thing . . . big heavy ball . . . he climbs in
  he says 'Where shall I start?'
  I said
  'That front bit
  that front bit where it happened

that bit in the front.'
And he hit it with the first swing
right by the window where
if she'd looked out
she might have seen us driving by
looking for . . .

A heavy crunch, metal against stone . . .

and the corner of the shed caved in
and I felt like it hit my chest . . .
and he went swinging at it again and again
and it all came down
within minutes
it was gone
it was like my heart torn out of my chest
and oh
there was nothing there any more
nothing at all
just nothingness.

A sound of splintering ice floes . . .

Oh
help
help
help.

Rhona!

Ingrid!

SIXTEEN: THE BRAINS OF IT

Agnetha
At this stage,
Dr David Nabkus, who is the neurologist in our
partnership . . .

Slight pause.

takes a detailed medical history.
In his absence . . .

Slight pause.

I will endeavour to find out
what he would find out . . .

She sits, Ralph circles round her. She watches him for a time.

You have a little limp there, Ralph . . .

Ralph
No.

Agnetha
Yes, I think so.

She watches him as he circles her . . . so he stands still, behind her.

Ralph.
Don't stand behind me.

Ralph
It frightens you.

Agnetha
No.
They stop us meeting if you . . .
Come in front of me.
Let me see this limp.

Ralph
No limp.

He walks to stand in front of her.

Agnetha
Mmmm.

Can you hop? On the right leg.
For just a little time?

Rolls his eyes because she is mad . . . but hops.

Agnetha
Good.
Now the left.

Ralph does so . . . staggers.
    Far away, something falls from a great height . . .
fractures . . .

Ralph
Shite!

Tries again.

Shite!
Pardon my French.

Agnetha
Okay.
You're just proving something for me.
No Big Deal.
Come sit down.
Talk to me.

Ralph sits down. Agnetha regards him . . . then leans
forward and goes to touch his forehead gently. Ralph
flinches back, swatting her. She flinches back.

Ralph
Sorry!

Agnetha
Sorry!

Ralph
Sorry.

Agnetha
Sorry.

Both look towards Guard.

Agnetha (*to Guard*)
Sorry.
(*to Ralph*)
I was just going to ask . . .
how did you get that scar?

Ralph (*touches it.*)
This.
Er.
I fell off a roof.
Blacked out.
Bosh.
I was pissed, pissed
and
I was getting away from somebody
and
bosh
just over and then whack
nothing broken
just like this bruise come up fucking large as an egg . . .

Agnetha
How old were you?

Ralph
'Bout . . . eighteen . . .
probably . . . yeah . . . no no no! . . . this was a car!
we got this car . . . and took it out for a burn yeah . . .
and whacked it into a wall yeah . . .
I wasn't driving
obviously
but I go smack! seat in front . . .

Agnetha

This was when you were . . .

Ralph

Sixteen?
blood all in my eye (*right eye*)
couldn't see fuck when we legged it!
but
hey . . .?
Give us your hand . . .

Agnetha (*to Guard.*)

I'm touching him, okay?
It's just investigative, okay?

Slowly she does . . .

Ralph

Feel there . . .

Agnetha

. . .
oh yes . . .
what happened there?

Ralph

I fell down a mine shaft!
I was blacked out for hours yeah . . .
was running
didn't see it just didn't see it . . .
bosh
trip
bosh
fall
whack
out!
It was serious because it was same place as
where my mam threw me in the sink . . .

Agnetha
When was this?
When your mom threw you in the sink?

Ralph
Oh
a kid
little
obviously . . .
when she could get away with it still!

The screen registers a table of figures as . . .

Agnetha
Over the years
Dr David Nabkus and myself have studied
more than 250 dangerous criminals . . .
in significant numbers,
these men have incurred physical damage to
the brain.
We have compiled a list of all the
verifiable brain injuries suffered by
fifteen randomly selected Death Row inmates . . .
as you will see from the paper . . .
page 5, table D . . .
the instances are many.

After Dr Nabkus has finished
his medical history . . .
I look for evidence of child abuse . . .

A sound of blustery wind . . .

SEVENTEEN: A LINE OF WASHING

Nancy, her kitchen garden, a pile of washing, a clothes line. March. Morning.

Nancy
  Instead of letters
  telling us where she was
  how she was getting along and whatnot
  these mucky little parcels start arriving
  inside
  cloth squares about this big . . .
  bright colours
  with foreign-type writing on . . .
  Handkerchiefs?
  Head squares?
  Then a postcard . . .
  'In Lhasa. Hope you got the Tibetan
  prayer flags.
  They are printed with spiritual blessings.
  They are hung up each year
  to signify
  hope
  transformation
  and the spreading of compassion. As the year progresses
  the wind disperses the energy of the words,
  which carry the power to pacify and heal
  everything they touch.
  Lots of love.

  Ingrid.'

Shoved them in my bits-and-bobs drawer.
Daft business.

Then . . . the trial starts to happen . . .

She starts pegging out.

I say
'Can I have our Rhona's remains so we can at least
    bury her . . . '
letter comes back . . .
Ralph Wantage's solicitor insists on keeping the remains
as his 'exhibits' . . .
I carry the letter with me all day . . .
it's on the bedside table all night.
I don't sleep.
I think I am as near to being not alive any more
as I've ever been.
I put the letter in my bits-and-bobs drawer
and there's those flag things.
I take them out
peg them on the line

What she has pegged out are the Tibetan prayer flags.
A wind waves them.

it's a damn windy day
they flap and flap and
the gate opens and
this thin, thin, brown thing head wrapped in a lot of
    cloth says
'Hello, Mum, it's me.
See you got the flags then?
Cool.'

Ingrid.
Ingrid.
Ingrid.

Agnetha, addressing her interested audience. Large,
comfortable lecture hall.

Agnetha
    My colleague
    Dr David Nabkus and I
    observed a group of toddlers over three months . . .
    half of whom had been subjected to
    serious physical abuse
    half of whom had not.
    We were interested in how the toddlers
    responded to a classmate in distress.
    What we found was that the healthy
    almost always responded to a crying or unhappy peer
    with concern and sadness
    or
    showed interest and made some attempt
    to provide comfort.
    But the abused toddlers *never* showed any concern.
    At most, they showed interest.
    The majority either got fearful and
    distressed themselves,
    or lashed out with threats, anger
    and physical assaults . . .

    Here is David's description of 'Martin'
    an abused boy of thirty-two months . . .

    She switches on the tape . . . sound of David Nabkus.
    We see her listening, watching.

David
    . . . he tries to take the hand of the crying
    other child, and when she resists, he slaps her
    on the arm with his open hand . . .

55

He then turns away from her to look at the ground
and begins vocalising very strongly . . .
'Cut it out!
CUT IT OUT! . . .'
each time saying it a little faster and louder.
He pats her
but she becomes disturbed by his patting . . .
so he retreats,
he hisses at her
he bares his teeth . . .
then he begins patting her on the back again
his patting becomes beating
and he continues beating her
even though she's screaming . . .

*Agnetha is with Ralph in the prison room. Tears are
coursing down her cheeks, sobs interrupting her
breathing. Ralph is watching her . . .*

Agnetha
Sorry.

Ralph
Stop.

Agnetha
Sorry . . . it's just . . .

Ralph
Stop that.

Agnetha
I'm sorry.
His voice is upsetting me a little . . .

*A Guard, impassive, responds to Agnetha's signs that
all is well. Ignores Ralph's agitation . . .*

Ralph
Just stop it
okay

okay
just stop it.

Agnetha
I'm sorry.
It's just . . . this man . . . a good friend of mine . . .
a colleague . . .
has died recently . . .
I'm sorry.
Where were we?

Ralph
You sit down.
You put your chair very close in to the table.
You open your legs as wide as they'll go.
Then I put my hand slowly slowly
down so Chummy over there
sees nothing
and I search with my fingers till they find
your pussy.
Your knickers are there . . .
so I go rip!
My finger ends are touching pussy now.
I find where you go in.
I position.
Then I ram in
obviously
again and again and again and again
oh yes
oh yes!

*Agnetha returns to her lectern. Footage of children
playing runs as . . .*

Agnetha
You see
the second critical argument in my thesis
is that child abuse

causes profound and pathological changes in
the structure of the brain as surely as injury does.
David and I brain-scanned the children
of severe neglect.
We found that entire structures of their cortex
never properly developed . . .
these cortical regions were twenty to thirty per cent
    smaller
than normal . . .

Abuse also disrupts the brain's stress response system
with profound results . . .
when something traumatic happens . . .
a fall from a roof . . .
a car accident . . .
a fight . . .
the brain responds by releasing
several waves of hormones . . .
the last of which is cortisol –

somewhere, some liquid starts dripping slowly . . .

– which is supposed to bring everything back
    to normal.
The problem is . . . cortisol is toxic . . .
if someone is exposed to too much stress
over too long a time . . .
all that cortisol begins to eat away at the organ
of the brain known as the hippocampus
which serves as the brain's archivist . . .
organising and shaping memories,
putting them in context
placing them in space and time
tying together visual memory with sound and smell.
J. Douglas Bremner, at Yale, has
measured this damage in controlled circumstance.
In those who had been abused,

Bremner found the hippocampus to be
on average twelve per cent smaller.
Abuse also affects the relationship between
the left hemisphere of the brain
which plays a large role in logic and language
and the right hemisphere,
which is thought to play a disproportionately large
role in creativity and depression.
Martin Teicher, at Harvard, recently gave an EEG
– the scan that measures electricity in the brain –
to 115 children admitted to a psychiatry facility
with a history of some kind of abuse . . .
not only was the rate of abnormal EEGs
twice as high as a non-abused group,
but in every case, the abnormality was on the left.
Instead of having two integrated hemispheres,
these patients have brains, in some sense,
divided down the middle.

A sound of something breaking . . .

What you get is a kind of erraticness . . .
they can be very different in one situation
compared to another . . .
there is a sense that they don't have a
larger moral compass . . .
in someone abused or neglected
the section of the brain involved
in attachment
in making emotional bonds
would actually look different
the wiring wouldn't be as dense, as complex.
They are literally lacking some brain organisation
that allows them to actually make strong connections
to other human beings . . .

Lights up once again on her and Ralph.

Ralph
Was I out of order then?

Agnetha
Yeah.
Sorta.
But it's okay, Ralph.
It's not your fault.
You can't help it.

NINETEEN: THE BONES OF IT

Nancy, smart outfit, sits on something low, unsuitable,
lights cigarette with quivering hand.

Nancy
Well.
Well.
Well.
. . . We've just come from the chapel of rest.
They still won't release her bones and . . .
I said 'I can't bear it, nothing's moving . . .'
and Ingrid says
in her new, quiet, calm . . . *round* . . . voice . . .
'Let's take some stuff down then . . .
our stuff . . .
give her some protection.

Just been
just now

I thought they'd refuse
red tape
sub judice etcetera
but no . . .
Mortician showed us straight into the chapel of rest.
Her coffin.

Ingrid says 'We've got some things, we'd like to put
them with her . . .'
I thought he'd draw the line at that,
get shirty, but no . . .
he takes a screwdriver out of his top pocket
unscrews the lid
takes it off and stands with it.
There's two cardboard boxes . . . different sizes . . .
DIY-archive system type . . . we've got them in the
    FLAME
office for files . . .
Ingrid points to the smaller one . . .
up the . . . up the head end . . .
and says 'Is this the skull?'
He nods.
'Go on,' she says to me, very quiet, 'open it.'

It's

it's

it's beautiful.

Sound of summer garden . . .

I take it out and hold it in my hands
and
I can feel her head
its shape and texture and . . .
resilience

and I'm *flooded* with its *joy*!!! . . .

Birdsong, summer insects buzz . . .

And I say to the mortician 'It's beautiful!'
and he just nods
because he knows it is.
Well, if anybody would know that he'd know that . . .
and after a while I give it to Ingrid

who says 'This fantastic brown it is,'
and she holds it here (*her heart*) for a long time
and then she puts Rhona's witch stone
with it back in the box
and closes the lid.

Bigger box.
Ingrid takes the lid off.

Different parts of her they managed to . . .
I thought top of the arm . . .
collar bone . . .
leg . . .

In there, we put a piece of gorse off
her nature table . . .
sheep wool wrapped in it . . .
place she *loved* to go to . . . windy hill . . .
daft really but . . .
also . . . Leo the Lion . . .
I go to the chap . . . 'Guard her, keep her safe,'
and we all smile.

And then . . . all the lids go back on.
He screws the lid back on the coffin
and I say
'Thank you,'
And he says 'No problem.
I wish more people could be doing this.'

She lights another cigarette. Agitated, angry, unsettled
as . . .

Then we come outside into this place.
Handy little parky garden place.
I feel at peace.
We're holding hands.
Me and . . . *bloody* Ingrid!!!

And she says . . .

'Now, Mum . . . Be In The Moment'
I say 'What, Petal?'
She says 'Mum . . .
You're in a Very Bad Space.
You've Got To Let Go Of Your Anger.
You've got to Move On.
If You Hold On To Your Rage,
It Will Consume You.
Let It Go.
Make Space for Other Things To Enter Your Heart.'
She's got this new way of talking . . .
It's like listening to a Diet and Exercise Book.
I said 'What do you want me to do?'
. . . (that's how you talk back to them . . .)
and she said . . .
'I think what we Have To Do
is Forgive Ralph Wantage With Our Whole Hearts.'

I said 'I want to slap you
I want to spit in your face
I want to scratch you
I want to tear your eyes out with my . . .'

She said 'She's been dead for twenty years.
It's long enough.

Let Her Go.'

I said 'I just did, in there.'

I couldn't bear to look at her.

She said 'You should go and see him.
Tell him you forgive him.'

I said 'If I go to see him,
I'm taking a gun.
Blow his brains all over the wall.
I'm taking a knife
slice his thing off

stick the blade through his eye
and take out his brains that thought
what he thought to do what he did . . .
She was my little girl!'

And she said

Pause.

'So was I.'

I can't do that.
I Can't Do That.
I CAN'T DO THAT!!!!!!!

End of Act One.

Act Two

TWENTY: A PHONE CALL HOME

*Agnetha, drink in one hand, cigarette in the other,
circling a telephone. She is thinking about phoning . . .
sometimes the decision is 'no', sometimes it is nearly
'yes' . . . then, finally, it is, 'fuck it, yes' . . .*

Agnetha
Hi . . .
Is that . . .
Mary?
. . . you sound like you're in a . . . *bathosphere* or
something! . . .
Do I? . . .
No . . . I'm just in *London* . . . (*English pronunciation*)
yeah . . . (*grand*) 'The *Brit* Lecture'!
yeah . . . the one David and I were gonna . . .
it's . . . well . . . *kinda weird* . . .
but . . . hey . . .
Listen . . . how you doing? . . .

She listens.

Well, you would . . . you will . . .
ah, Mary . . . I know . . . I know . . .
but . . .

She listens.

Mary . . . you just hafta be kind to yourself . . .
and . . . give yourself treats . . . and . . .
keep warm . . .
and . . . make everybody else look after you . . .
Even *The Kids!*
How are the . . .?

Give 'em a kiss from me, okay?
Hell . . . give em *two!*

She takes a deep breath and . . .

Listen, Mary . . .
I've done a dumb thing . . .
I got drunk and . . .
I know I don't . . . I don't smoke either . . . that's
the *peculiar* thing . . .
but okay, I got . . . *major pie-eyed* and I . . .
sent an e-mail to David

and I'm frightened you got it.

Oh
you . . .
listen . . . I'm *really* sor . . .
you must have . . .
I have to . . .
Whaddya mean it made you *laugh*? . . .
Mary!!!!!
Another woman sends your dead husband a
piece of *hate* mail and
you *laugh*?????
What kinda woman *are* you?

(*Beat.*) So it didn't make you . . .
You didn't get . . .

Listens really hard . . .

It's just . . .
Mary . . . I really miss him.

I played some footage of him
and . . . oh

yeah . . . with The Vicious Haircut . . .

Mary . . . you know I love you . . .

She listens.

Do you . . .?

She shakes her head . . .

Thank you . . .
that's . . .

Agnetha, away from the phone, bends over in agony.
Straightens, deep breath, and then . . .

I . . .
no, never mind . . .
listen . . .
I'll come see you when I get . . .

No . . . I haven't *met* anyone . . .
apart from serial killers . . .
This Brit Killer made me an offer I could refuse . . .
but hey, he's not dating at the present moment . . .
(*Listens.*) . . . Sure he's crazy . . .

Anything else happening with me . . .?

Mary . . .

Mary . . .

She lifts up her hand. The fingers are crossed.

Someone's just come in the room.
I gotta go . . .
okay! . . .
yeah!

Right!
Take care!

Phone replaced. Pause. She watches as Nancy walks
into a room somewhere.

Take care.

Agnetha, leaving her personal detritus, assuming an authoritative demeanour, walks into the same room as Nancy . . .

TWENTY-ONE: TWO CARING WOMEN MEET

Nancy
I want to meet him.

I *have* to now

to . . .

Her hand makes the sign of 'go straight forward'.

He

She has to do this.

took her
she was going to Grandma's for me . . .
and he forced her into the van
and
she's ten
and
and he . . .
then he wrapped her in polythene sheeting
she was unconscious
but she wasn't dead then
he took her to a *shed* near
and
we *think* he sexually assaulted her
before he held the polythene on her face
and suffocated her.

She is short of breath.

Agnetha
Breathe.

Both inhale and exhale, hands on breasts, Nancy sort
of following Agnetha . . .

Nancy
 I'm accepting it.
 I'm accepting she's dead.
 But

Pause.
   Somehow an awful admission of guilt.

 I'm not

 and I need to

The same hand gesture of moving forward . . .

 so
 he's the next step.

 I want to know *why.*
 I want to know why *her.*
 I want him to know what he's done.
 I want him to know how I *feel.*
 I want to *understand.*
 If I could understand *why* . . . I might feel . . .
 it might be . . . *better* . . . or even just bloody
 different . . .
 I might be able to . . .

For the third time, the hand gesture.

 I've read all the data vis-a-vis the use of
 Victim–Offender Communication in the
 Treatment of Sexual Abuse and
 Violent Crime Trauma . . .
 My organisation is monitoring all the
 Victim-Sensitive Offender Schemes Stateside . . .
 Research-wise I'm impeccably prepared.
 I think my letters state that I'm up to
 speed.

They said you could help.
Rubber-Stamp It.
Fast-Track It.
It's Time.
I want a visit.

*Agnetha stands. Walks to the coffee machine,
thinking. Looks back at Nancy.*

Agnetha
Coffee?

*Nancy shakes her head. Agnetha pours two cups and
carries them into the next scene for . . .*

TWENTY-TWO: MY CHILDHOOD

*Ralph and Agnetha, cup of hot coffee each. Sort of both
off-duty. Guard still there.*

Ralph
. . . no . . . my *video* collection was in the *back* of the
    shed . . .
my . . . the *girls* were in the main body of the
    building . . .

Agnetha
but . . . *everything* . . . wrapped in polythene . . . right?

Ralph
Oh yes
oh yes.

Agnetha
And . . . filed?

Ralph
Obviously
everything was in order
the whole lay-out made sense

if they'd *asked* me I'd've taken them through it
methodically . . .
they needn't have . . .
going in mobhanded . . . they destroyed . . . the videos . . .
you're looking at about three thousand quid . . .

Agnetha
. . . but you see their point, Ralph . . .

Ralph
Oh yes still
coulda been more *organised.*

Agnetha
No *remorse* then, Ralphie?

Ralph
Remorse. So what is that . . . remorse?

Agnetha
Like Regret. But more.
It's a feeling of . . . *compunction* . . .
of . . . deep . . . *regret* . . .
you *repent* your sin . . .
last cookie . . .

Ralph
Last what?

Agnetha
Last . . . (*remembers word*) . . . *biscuit* . . . last
    biscuit . . . split it?

*Ralph nods. She splits the last biscuit and they share
it as . . .*

You feel . . .
sorrow
pity
compassion . . .
a sort of . . . *tender* feeling . . . in . . . (*heart*) . . . here.

Ralph
I can't say I do.

Pause. Thinks.

The only thing I'm sorry about is that
it's not legal.

Agnetha
What's not legal?

Ralph
Killing girls.

*Agnetha looks at her watch, picks up her writing pad,
switches on her tape . . . business again.*

Agnetha
Tell me about killing girls, Ralph.

Ralph
No.
It's Private.

Pause.

Agnetha
Tell me about your childhood then, Ralph.

Ralph
Big kitchen . . . we had a big kitchen obviously . . .
with an *Aga* . . . a dark green Aga . . . and that's
    where all
the kettles and pans . . . copper, all copper, all gleaming
in the light . . . because there were lights everywhere . . .
spotlights on tracking yeah . . . to just touch in a mood
of country . . . and a log fire . . . with them . . .
    whatsis . . . *settles* . . .
wood . . . pine . . . antiquey . . . and here is where
    the dog sits . . .

lies . . . when he's not guarding . . . or going out on
  the hills
with us, *romping* . . . and then we come back and
  open the
tin of Pal Pedigree dogfood and he gets it, bosh, in
a special new shiny tin on the red stone floor . . .

Agnetha
What kind of dog is he, Ralph?

Ralph
Golden retriever.
Pedigree. Kennel Club obviously.

Agnetha
What's his name?

Ralph (*pause*)
He doesn't have a name.
We don't go in for names.

Pause.

Lassie.

Agnetha
Tell me about your parents.

Ralph
Mother does the meals.
She goes to Iceland and Sainsbury's and Tesco's
and she gets a *variety* and she doesn't put up with
low standards . . .
oh no
oh no
the long pine table *always* has a selection of
. . . and the *correct* cutlery crockery for different
meals . . . and we all sit down to eat together . . .

Agnetha
And what does . . . Mother . . . cook for you all?

Ralph
Steakmasters . . . Oven Cook Chips . . . Viennettas . . .
After Dinner Mints . . . Hamlet Cigars . . .
Crusty Warm Bread . . .
Haagen-Daz ice cream any many flavours . . . Mixed
Grills . . .

Agnetha
Is Father there?

Ralph
Yeah. Father. *Dad.*
Except when we're out riding ponies.
Or reading *poytry*.
In the room with all the books on shelves.
And the Nicam Digital television.

Agnetha
Any brothers or sisters, Ralph?

Ralph
No.
I'm an only child.
A much-loved only child.
Spoilt rotten.
But what can I do?

Agnetha (*she regards him for a time*)
Childhood's kinda private too, huh, Ralph?

Ralph
Yes
oh yes.

*She picks up the biscuit plate. Crumbs on it. Carries
it out past the Guard.*

Agnetha
But we know you're a liar, Ralph.
And inconsistent.
We got a few crumbs from you.

74

She moistens a forefinger, starts picking up the biscuit crumbs, eating them, as . . .

Little bits of you, cookie!
Your mom pops you in the sink
step dads arrive
you get chased
you get fucked
up your little bottom, don't you?
up your sad, dirty little ass . . .
We're onto you,
you sad, predictable, banal
fuck . . .

She realises she is eating his crumbs. She retches as . . .

'Memo.
Restorative Justice Lobby.
I would not be comfortable in
recommending Mrs Nancy Shirley
visit Ralph Wantage . . .'

TWENTY-THREE: THE SACRED ART OF FENG-SHUI

Nancy, paint-spattered clothes . . . a splodge of white paint ludicrously across her face.

Nancy
Drip-Free Paint!
Liars!

It's big, this room
with everything out of it
spacious.

You can swing a cat in here now . . .

I'd swing that bloody American Doctor woman round
by her . . .

(*Quotes.*)
'The *experiment* is unviable!
The components *unstable!*'
Who does she think she *is*?

I've written some letters
made some phone calls
that's what you learn if you run an organisation . . .
Use The Right People!

I'll get that visit!

Whole house is bigger now . . .
Rhona's kiddie furniture gone
Bob's stuff . . .
I left a message saying 'Will I drop your stuff round?'
but he's lying low.
Sulking.

Only Ingrid speaks to me.

Nobody else.

They think what I want to do is . . . criminal . . .

Laughs.

So much for Families.

Doesn't matter.

Bob was Yesterday's Newspapers for me anyway.

I said 'I'm sorry, but how I felt about you
just hasn't survived . . .
it didn't keep . . . like something in the fridge . . .
    a leftover . . .
in a jar . . . and when I picked it up . . . it was empty . . .'
and he said 'Don't get *descriptive* with *me*!
I could have set up with Marie from Nautilus
. . . why leave it till I'm nearly bloody *Past It*????'
I said 'Revenge, probably' . . . but I don't mean that.

I don't mean him no harm.
I've got no malice in me.
No nothing.

Just	space
for	
something	fresh
bit of	light
in the	red
bit of	fresh air
new	feelings. (*It hurts.*)
Once this visit's . . .	I might go somewhere

I don't need to be here
nothing's keeping me

I'm free to go.

Sound of wings fluttering, not birds . . .
    Some beautiful music plays . . .

TWENTY-FOUR: CONCLUDING MY ADDRESS

Agnetha at the lectern . . . large hall.

Agnetha
I spoke, in my preamble
of myself as explorer . . .
of . . . navigating
the Arctic frozen sea of the criminal brain . . .
Well the expedition is complete.
What discoveries do we bring back from that foreign
    terrain
to help make our own inner and outer landscape
warmer safer kinder better?
You see . . .

I just don't believe people are born evil.
To my mind that is mindless.
Forensic psychiatrists tend to buy into the notion
of evil.
But I feel that that's no explanation.
The deed itself is bizarre, grotesque.
But it's not evil.
To my mind evil bespeaks conscious control
over something.
Serial murderers are not in that category.
They are driven by forces beyond their control.
The difference between a crime of evil
and a crime of illness is the difference
between a sin and a symptom
And symptoms do not intrude in the relationship
    between
murderers and the rest of us.
They do not force us to stop and observe the
distinctions between right and wrong,
between the speakable and unspeakable,
the way sins do . . .

Agnetha moves away from the lectern . . .

But when you get back
and you're cold
you're freezing yourself . . .
you've got snow in your head instead of . . .
warmth
clarity.
What then, Doctor Gottsmundottir . . .
What then?
If it's snowing excuses explanations justifications
don't you cease to be an explorer
and start . . .
living there?

Prison visiting room. Ralph seated, Nancy at the entrance. A Guard.

Nancy (*to Guard*)
That's him?

Guard nods . . . she goes to stand in front of Ralph.

Ralph Wantage?

Ralph looks up. Barely nods.

Nancy Shirley.
You got my letter.
You agreed to see me.
Shall I sit down?

She does. For a long time, they look, they really look, at one another . . .

Ralph
She was your kid . . .
One of them.
This . . .

Nancy
Rhona.

Ralph
Rhona.
Funny you coming.

Pause. Ralph sits. Nancy sits.

Nancy
I want you to know
I forgive you for killing my daughter.

Silence. Ralph abruptly covers his eye sockets with

both hands. Long pause. Guard watches Ralph.
Nancy glances at Guard. Then Nancy sits down.
Ralph brings his hands down, looks somewhere at
the corner of her.
   Very long pause . . . then the words sound very
rusty . . .

Ralph
   Thank you.

   They sit for a time.

   It's a nice day anyway.

Nancy
   Yes.
   There's buds out.
   We saw a great *bank* of pussy willow on the way here.
   I should have brought you some.
   Are you allowed . . . that sort of thing?

   He ignores her. He has no idea if he is allowed that
   sort of thing. Both glance at Guard. Guard nods.
   They both look away.

Ralph
   We can have videos now.

Nancy
   That's nice.
   Is that nice?

Ralph
   It's alright.

   Long pause.

Nancy
   I want you to know
   I don't hate you.

Ralph
  Okay.

Nancy
  I used to.
  But I don't any more.

Ralph
  Okay.

Nancy
  My daughter . . . Ingrid . . . said . . . Let It Go . . .
  Like A Bird Into The Wind.
  She's Spiritual.

Ralph
  How old is she?

Nancy
  Thirty-seven.

Ralph
  Oh.

  He is not interested.

Nancy
  I've brought some photographs.
  Would you like to see them?

Ralph
  Of . . . her?

Nancy
  Rhona.
  And our family. Ingrid. Bob. My husband.

  She gets them out. A small dog-eared selection.

  That's Rhona as a baby.

  Hands them to him in turn.

That's me holding her.
This is Ingrid, that's her sister, holding her.
This is them holding their pets.
Her cat is Fluff
Ingrid's holding Black-and-White.
You can see why they're called that . . . because she's
fluffy . . . and he's . . . see . . .?
This is Rhona with Ingrid and my husband Bob.
We were on a day out.
I took it . . . it's uneven ground . . .
that's why they're slightly . . .

Her body indicates leaning . . .

This is Rhona dressed as an octopus.
For a fancy-dress competition.

Ralph
Did she win?

Nancy
She came third.
Behind Little Miss Muffet
and a Loch Ness Monster.

She points them out.

Ralph
She should have won.

Nancy
That's what we thought.
But we were biased obviously.

Ralph
That's good those arms.
How did you do them?

Nancy
She did them.
Rhona.

They're wire she made into springs.
When you touched them,
they . . .

Body language shivers and vibrates . . .

Ralph
I don't think I hurt her.

Nancy
You did.

Ralph
I don't think she was frightened at all . . .

Nancy
She must have been.

Ralph thinks for a long time. Nancy watches him carefully. When he looks up suddenly, she holds his gaze. He looks away . . . she touches his arm . . .

Ralph
You're not allowed to touch.

Nancy
Sorry.

Guard is watching. She removes her hand. Both sit back.

Nancy
But she must have been frightened!

Ralph keeps thinking . . .

Ralph
Do you live on a farm
and ride horses
and read poytry
and have warm bread?

Nancy
Not on a farm.

No horses.
We aren't particular big on poetry.
Books, though.
Yes. Sometimes. Warm bread.
On cold days. You just pop it in the oven on
a low heat. Few minutes . . .

Ralph nods. He knew this.

Did your mother ever . . .?

Ralph
Oh yes.
Oh yes. (*She didn't.*)

Nancy
And your dad? What did he do?

Ralph
My dad
well
he was the disciplinarian
obviously.

Nancy
Made you behave, did he?

Ralph
Oh yes
oh yes.
Say you swore filthy language
he's got you by the hair here (*back of neck*)
and you're in the washing up water
bosh, wash your mouth out with soap water!
or you done wrong
anything!
he's
(*in Dad's voice*) See my eyes, twat?
Can you see it, you fucking little pillock?
I'm looking into you and I'm seeing shit!

You hear me?

Sound of a thump on flesh . . . Ralph registers it, side of head.

You deaf little bugger!

Another thump, same side of head. Ralph's body registers it.

You listening to me?
Your head (*tap on forehead*) taking this in?
I'll make sure you hear what I say . . .
Stand still
stand still
stand still
you stand still and don't move one muscle
not one
you don't even blink, twat
until I know you know I mean what I say.

'See my eyes, twat?'

Ralph is blinking rapidly.

Nancy
Frightening bugger.

Ralph nods

Hurt you a lot.

Ralph, after a time, nods

Can you see it hurt Rhona then?
Can you see it frightened her?
What you did.

Ralph thinks impassive for a long time. Then . . .

Ralph
Yes.

He nods.
  Nods more times.
  Tears in his eyes.
  He wipes them fiercely. Violently.
  Dry painful sobs start.
  Awful, embarrassing, rusty crying.

Nancy watches. Guard watches. He holds his chest
in pain as he subsides. Calmly, she takes out a tissue.
Holds it up to Guard questioningly. He nods slightly,
dismissively. Nancy hands it to Ralph. He uses it. Puts
it on the table between them. Guard watches.

Ralph
Don't come and bother me again.
Cunt.

A pause. Then, a genuine apology . . .

Scuse my French.

TWENTY-SIX: ODE TO JOY

Agnetha, tidying up her paperwork, laptop, detritus,
clothing . . . packing . . . She is humming . . . At some
point, it turns into a full production number, with
Agnetha on lead vocals, backing vocals, wind, string and
brass section . . .

Agnetha
  . . . doo doo doo . . .
  Pardon me boy . . .
  is that the Chattanooga choo choo?
  track twenty-nine . . .
  well, you can gimme a shine . . .
  You leave the
  Pennsylvania station 'bout a quarter to four
  read a magazine and then

you're in Baltimore
dinner in the diner
nothing could be finer
than to have your ham and eggs
in Carolina.
When you hear the whistle blowing
eight to the bar
then you know that . . . where the fuck? is not very far

Shovel all the coal in
gotta keep 'em rolling
choo choo Carolina
here we are . . .

There's gonna be . . .
a certain party at the station . . .

Who you kidding?

Satin and lace
I used to call funny face . . .

Who you kidding, Sad Woman . . .?
there's gonna be ice . . .
ice as far as the eye can see . . .
ice ice ice
and perpetual night! . . .

TWENTY-SEVEN: LETTER-WRITING

*Ralph, communal area, writing . . . interruptive loud
music playing off centre.*

Ralph
Dear Mrs Shirley . . .
Dear Nancy . . .
Dear Mrs Shirley . . .
I am writing to you . . .

I am sorry . . .
I am *very* sorry . . .
I am sorry . . .
I am sorry that I murdered . . .
I am sorry that I abused . . .
I am sorry that I . . .

Turn the *fucking* music!!!!!
Turn the *fucking* noise down!!!!!
You . . . Fuck! . . . Down!!!!!

Down!

Bit of fucking *peace* . . . Jesus!

*He aligns his stationery and pens into neatness. And
again. And again.*

I am sorry.
I am sorry from the bottom of my heart.

I am thinking about what I did.

I am thinking about what I did.

I am realising.

I realise in abusing and killing your daughter

. . . *Rhona* . . .

I hurt her.

You

*He realigns the paper . . . pen . . . envelope. And
again.*

Oh Christ.

*He spits on the paper, folds it carefully, puts it in the
envelope. Seals it. Tears it up. He starts to collect and
align the torn pieces into a pile as . . .*

Fucking Music!

TWENTY-EIGHT: SOMETHING AWFUL

Nancy, a cup of morning tea, a dressing gown . . .
a sachet of 'Resolve'.

Nancy
Well!
Well!
Well . . . I'll go to the foot of our stairs!
Nancy Shirley!
Nancy Shirley, how could you?
I've just done something *awful*!
I've been out on a DATE!
With a *Man*!
Roy Taylor!
Roy Taylor!
To a *Chinese Restaurant!*
Mince in *lettuce* leaves you eat with your fingers
and prawns in ginger and . . .
all this *washed down* with some sort of
oriental wine
and I get tiddly and
you know what's coming next
he says 'Can I come in for a bit'
and I say 'Lovely'
and next thing we're up there
doing . . . well . . . you can imagine!

Ingrid dropped by with this . . .
. . . 'Remorse' . . .

Looks closer.

. . . 'Resolve' . . . Resolve . . .

Ingrid says she understands.

Which is more than I do!

She says 'It's The Life Force.'

The Wine Talking more like!

I said 'This isn't *me* . . . Ingrid . . .'

She said 'He's not bad looking . . .'

I said '*Please* don't tell your father!'

Life Force!

She talks such . . . *hocus pocus*!

TWENTY-NINE: QUIET AND SILENCE

*Agnetha and Ralph, prison room . . . a tape recorder . . .
notes. Agnetha closes her notebook.*

Agnetha
Well, Ralph. This is my last visit.
I wondered if you wanted to tell me anything more.
And I came to say 'Goodbye'.

Ralph
Can you turn that thing off? (*tape*)
I've been wanting to tell you things I
don't want recorded, yeah?

Agnetha
Okay.

Turns off the tape.

Yes?

Ralph
I think I've caught something.
I think I caught cancer or something.
Here.
That's lungs, right?

Lung cancer.
And that's me not even fucking smoking!

Agnetha
What does the doctor say?

Ralph
Says it's just Stress!
Fucking Shite!
Stress is in here. (*forehead*) I know where
Fucking Stress Is!
This fucking *gnawing*, here! (*chest*)
Not Fucking Stress!

Agnetha
Where is this pain, Ralph?

He shows her.

That's your heart, Ralph.
Did the doctor check out your heart?

Ralph
Says there's nothing fucking *wrong*
with the heart!
Fucking Quack Cunt!

Agnetha
How long have you been in pain, Ralph?

Ralph
Er . . .
It started . . . night after that mother of that
girl Rhona I done came . . . that was Thursday . . .
so . . . (*Counts on his fingers.*)
It's been a bit.

Agnetha
Mrs Shirley came to see you?
I recommended she . . .

Ralph

Yes, well . . . you were overruled by
The Doctor-in-Charge of Nutting-Off
weren't you?

Agnetha

And she visited with you?

Ralph

Yes.
She's forgive me, actually.
We're straight on it.

Spasm in his chest.

Oya
Oya
Oya.

Agnetha

I think you should talk to your doctor again.
Ask to see a psychologist.
What you are feeling may be psychological.
What you are feeling may be
Remorse.
And that will be very painful for you
Ralph.
Try rub it . . . here.

*She shows him on herself . . . middle of the chest, just
below the sternum.*

Ralph

Fucking hurts.
Burns.
Eats.
Gnaws.
Fucking Cancer.

Agnetha

Well. I'm sorry.

I hope they find out what it is and . . .
sort it out.
So.
This is goodbye.

She stands.

Take care.

*Ralph tidies and realigns everything on the table top.
And again. And again.*

Ralph
It's a question of finding a window
of opportunity
of always being ready
of always doing research
of committing yourself to
the rehearsal
the training
for practising
for when that
one golden moment
shines.

Agnetha looks at the Guard.

Agnetha
I'm going to hug him goodbye.
Sue me.

*She gently puts her arms round Ralph and gives him a
hug. Kisses him on the cheek.*

Bye, Ralph.

*She walks away from him. She hears somewhere
beautiful, haunting music playing as . . .
    He starts to take off his shirt, pullover . . . folds
them neatly . . . as . . .*

THIRTY: FAREWELL TO LONDON

Agnetha, her living accommodation, London. Checking her airline tickets, passport . . .

Agnetha
Yes
yes
yup
yeah
yo.

All is ready. She looks around.

Bye London.

She feels relief.

Yesssssss!

England. Goodbye.

She feels more relief.

Yeeeesssssssssss!

Weird England. 'Toodle-pip.'

She experiences elation.

Hello . . . Iceland!
Yesssssssssss!!!!!!!!!!

She picks up her stuff to leave. Phone begins to ring somewhere. Goes to answer it as . . .

THIRTY-ONE: HOW HE DOES IT, WHY HE DOES IT

Ralph, in his cell, sweating, training gear. Working out.

Ralph
It's all a question of energy expended
vee calorie intake, yeah?
Fitness is what it's all about
which is twenty per cent genetic
and eighty per cent working at it yourself.
You can beat any condition if
you got a healthy body.
Oh yes
oh yes
fifteen
sixteen
seventeen eighteen
nineteen
twenty
yes!!!!

*He drops. Unwinds a long cloth from round his neck.
Wipes the sweat from his brow, body. One of his
tattoos catches his eye. Looks at it carefully, fondly.*

Angels Fighting Devils.

Goes to a chair. Sits in it.

Fucking craftsman.

*He stands up, slings the cloth over the pull-up bar.
With his belt he fashions a noose. Stands on his chair.*

Gnawed to death?
I don't think so.

*He completes his preparations. Kicks the chair away
from him. He hangs, choking, jerking as . . .*

Hello.
Hello.
Hello.
Hell . . .
He . . .

A burst of wild, beautiful music plays . . .

THIRTY-TWO: GRAVESIDE

Nancy, in a memorial garden. Some churchlike music off to the side comes to an end.
Agnetha, entering, watches her for a few seconds.

Agnetha
That's pretty . . .
The white one . . .

Nancy
Alchemilla.
It *is* a mess!

A pause. Nancy unhelpful.

Agnetha
Not a *big* funeral . . .

Nancy
Bit of a surprise . . . person with his talent for putting sunshine in everybody's life . . .

Agnetha
I think the old lady in the black fur was his mother . . .

Nancy
His foster mother.

Agnetha
She looked . . . bad . . .

Nancy
Not as bad as if she had been his mother . . .

Agnetha thinks about this.

Agnetha
Yes. Yes.
I think that would be unbearable.

Nancy
Actually, nothing's unbearable.

Agnetha
You came to see him.

Nancy
And you tried to stop me.

Agnetha
I was trying to protect everybody.

Nancy
Him.

Agnetha
Everybody.

Nancy
Him.
How much time and energy did you give him?
And me?
And the others?
Cigarette?

Agnetha (*wants to, but . . .*)
I'm trying not to . . .

Nancy
Me too. (*Puts hers away too.*)
You look upset.
Were you fond of Ralph?

Agnetha
It's not for Ralph . . .
It's for somebody else.
For me.

Nancy
Me as well.
I couldn't feel much for him really . . .

Agnetha
No.
It was . . .
not easy.

Both nod thoughtfully.

Nancy
Do you think he did it . . .
the . . . suicide . . .
Ralph . . .
because I came to see him . . .?

Long silence.

Agnetha
Yes.

Long silence.

Nancy
I don't know whether to be sad or glad.

Agnetha
Be both.

Nancy
No.
Bugger it.
I've been sad enough.
I'll be glad.
That murdering bugger's kept me from

happiness
and . . . laughing
and
cheer
for bloody twenty-odd years . . .
Bugger it.
Glad.
Laugh.
Have a joke.

Agnetha
My colleague and best friend,
David . . .
told jokes . . .

Nancy
Does he?

Agnetha
Did. Told. He died six months ago . . .
horribly . . .
stupid accident . . .
wearing a seat belt . . .
observing the speed limit . . .
a truck goes out of control . . .
the driver is on crack . . .
the truck smashes the car . . .
David . . .
the truck driver is unhurt.

Nancy takes Agnetha's hand. Very matter-of-fact.

Anyhow.
Good joke from him.
These two lovers decide to commit suicide.
They both work in the same office.
So they put arsenic in their sandwiches
go to work
twelve thirty

they eat them.
It's a Suicide Pact Lunch.

Both women smile . . . laugh?

Nancy (*acknowledges*)
Suicide Pact Lunch.

Agnetha
I worked with him every day for ten years.
Two days before he died . . .
I slept with him.

It just happened.

His wife is a very good friend.

Why am I telling you this?

Nancy
Why are you?

Agnetha
Do I tell her?

Nancy
No.
You just suffer.

'The difference between a crime of evil
and a crime of illness is the difference
between a sin and a symptom . . .'

Your words.

I read your thesis . . .

You knew what you were doing.
Live with it.

*Near, the sound of doleful funereal music from the
crematorium chapel.*

Oh, perfect.
Another funeral . . .!

The sun breaks through, birds twitter, music plays,
Nancy smiles at Agnetha.

The End.